The

Mental Health

Of the Leader

Nurturing Wholeness and Resilience

By Dr. Dwayne C. Perry

Dedicated to all the devoted leaders entrusted with the sacred duty of guiding others, may this book be a vessel of wisdom, inspiration, and spiritual growth to aid you in fulfilling your divine calling.

May the presence of the Holy Spirit empower and guide you as you develop into the exemplary leader you are destined to be, impacting and shaping the lives of those under your care for generations to come.

Acknowledgment

As I share my thoughts on mental health, I am filled with gratitude for those who have supported me along the way. This book would not have been possible without the encouragement, love, and wisdom of many individuals who have played crucial roles in my life.

Together, we can break the stigma surrounding mental health and foster a world where everyone feels seen, heard, and valued.

With gratitude,

Dr. Dwayne C. Perry

Introduction

In the world of power and influence, a hidden battle rages- one that is often masked by silence and stigma. It's a struggle with mental health that affects even the most prominent leaders. We've all seen the headlines about CEOs and politicians, but the untold stories behind those headlines are even more disturbing.

Take the story of Sandeep Rehal, the former CEO of a major tech company. His tragic battle with depression ended with him taking his own life.[1] Then there's Jacinda Ardern, the New Zealand Prime Minister, who shocked the world by stepping down, citing burnout and emotional exhaustion.[2]

But it's not just in the boardrooms and political arenas. Even religious leaders, who are often seen as beacons of hope and moral guidance, face their own silent struggles. Apostles, Pastors, and Bishops alike are vulnerable to the relentless pressures of their roles. The tragic death of Pastor Andrew Stoecklein of Inland Hills Church, who succumbed to suicide after battling anxiety and depression, shocked congregations and highlighted the mental health crisis within religious leadership.[3] Pastor Jarrid Wilson, known for his advocacy on mental health issues within the church, also tragically took his own life,

Table of Contents

leaving behind a moving message about the dire need for support and understanding in faith communities.[4]

These stories remind us of the enormous pressure that leaders face. They're expected to be strong and unwavering, but the reality is far from that. The stress and isolation that come with leadership can take a heavy toll on mental health. It's time to break the silence!

Leaders must recognize that their strength is not just in their decisions but also in their ability to seek help and care for their mental faculties. I've seen a lot and felt even more during my tenure in Leadership (Apostolic and Educational). Personally, I've struggled with feelings of isolation and inadequacy. I've come to understand that many leaders are spiritually gifted but emotionally immature, and this impacts their ability to navigate their own mental frustrations. I believe that having a framework of strategies is essential. **This book will provide that framework**.

A framework is essential.

Leadership, especially in apostolic settings, demands more than vision and strategy—it requires emotional maturity, spiritual resilience, and a commitment to personal well-being. Journey with me as we explore the mental well-being of leaders, incorporating scriptural references and insights from theologians, past and present. By understanding the various factors influencing mental health, we can better support and nurture our leaders. By taking a holistic approach, we can empower leaders to fulfill their calling with clarity and emotional stability.

Chapter 1- Mental Health & Apostolic Leadership

Leadership often comes with a silent battle—a struggle to maintain emotional balance while carrying the weight of responsibility. Mental health is a critical aspect of overall well-being, affecting individuals from all walks of life. Leaders are at the top of the list of those impacted. The bigger issue is that *"they can't admit it."* Many leaders are spiritually gifted but lack the emotional tools to handle their mental struggles. Apostolic leaders, in particular, face unique challenges that can impact their mental health. **What do I mean by Apostolic Leaders?** Let me start by sharing what I don't mean. I'm not referring to the title or office of an Apostle. What I mean is the Apostolic

Apostolic-
One who is sent,
who has a mandate
to go and establish;
A Pioneer.

Work. Apostolic refers to one who is sent, one who has a mandate to go and establish, and one who is a pioneer. Hereafter, when I use "Leader" I am referring to this particular type of leader. Apostolic work often requires trailblazing, going against the norm, and isolation. Because of this, mental health is greatly challenged. They carry a significant burden of responsibility, often serving as spiritual guides, counselors, and mentors to their communities. This weight of responsibility can lead to increased stress, anxiety, and emotional exhaustion. I am a leader who travels in this lane, so as I'm writing to "you", I am speaking to me.

Scripture and Theologian Insights

Throughout this book, we will explore how scripture and theologians weigh in on each topic. For example, Jesus Himself experienced moments of distress and sought solace in prayer (Matthew 26:36-46). The Psalms contain numerous passages that express emotions such as despair, anger, and sadness, providing solace and validation for those experiencing similar feelings. Likewise, leaders may experience feelings of isolation and loneliness due to the unique nature of our role. We often bear the weight of others' burdens while having limited outlets for sharing our own struggles. The Apostle Paul, in his letters, expressed feelings of loneliness and the need for companionship (2 Timothy 4:9-11). Passages such as Philippians 4:6-7 encourage believers to present their anxieties to God. The story of Elijah in 1 Kings 19 demonstrates the significance of mental health, as God addresses Elijah's emotional distress and provides him with rest and nourishment.

Leaders are targeted explicitly for spiritual warfare and may face intense spiritual battles that can impact our mental well-being. The Apostle Peter warns of the devil's schemes and encourages believers to remain vigilant (1 Peter 5:8-9). Throughout history, theologians have also recognized the significance of mental health within religious leadership. The works of theologians such as Augustine, Aquinas, and Bonhoeffer provide insights into the relationship between mental health and spirituality. These theologians emphasize the importance of self-reflection, community support, and the integration of faith and reason in promoting mental well-being. Theologian C.S. Lewis emphasizes the reality of spiritual warfare and the need for spiritual discernment and resilience. Recognizing the spiritual dimension of mental health is crucial in supporting leaders in their battles against discouragement and spiritual attacks.

I recall my battle. There was no space for my own trauma. I was dealing with my family, spouse, ex, and ex- extended family. I was also dealing with my church, the individuals and families that came along with it, and everybody else's ideologies and beliefs. At the end of the day, I was responsible. The question was, where do I go? I couldn't go to everybody because not everyone could handle that conversation. As a leader, I couldn't go to my parishioners because they looked up to me. Have you been there? It was crucial to find a person I could trust to have these honest, heartfelt conversations about my emotional state and struggles. But where was this resource? It wasn't easy to find, hence my urgency to produce this work.

The Question: As a Leader, Where do I Go?

Mental Strain Because of the Apostolic Work

A major arm of the Apostolic work involves Kingdom expansion. Here, leaders are charged with forging building projects, planting churches, and saturating the marketplace with God's agenda. Personally, I've experienced intense warfare in this arena. Three years ago, we made a significant investment by purchasing a property for $250,000. Today, that property has appreciated significantly and is now valued at an impressive $1.5 million. This remarkable increase in value is a testament to the strategic decisions and efforts we have put into the property. However, this journey has not been without its challenges.

Since the acquisition, the property owner's association has made numerous attempts to disregard the original agreement made during the purchase. These attempts have created an environment of conflict and tension, straining our operations and testing our resilience.

Moreover, my personal character and the integrity of our ministry have come under attack. These baseless accusations and efforts to undermine us have been deeply hurtful and challenging. Yet, it is in these very trials that I have found an unexpected blessing.

Through all the difficulties, my faith has been profoundly strengthened. Each obstacle has reinforced my calling and commitment to God's service. I have learned to lean on His wisdom and grace more than ever. The adversities faced have not only fortified my spiritual resolve but also provided me with invaluable lessons in perseverance and trust in God's plan.

Additionally, these experiences have afforded me a deeper understanding and greater insight into the complexities of dealing with commercial real estate. Navigating through legal disputes, handling conflicts, and managing property investments have honed my skills and broadened my expertise in this field. This knowledge will undoubtedly serve us well in future ventures and endeavors. More importantly, this challenge awakened me to the need to develop a framework for managing mental health in the leadership space.

Let's see what the scriptures and theologians have to say: Paul's letters to the early Christian communities often addressed emotional and psychological challenges, offering guidance and encouragement. In 2 Corinthians 1:3-4, Paul highlights the comfort he received from God during his own hardships, emphasizing the importance of supporting one another in times of distress.

The works of theologians such as Dietrich Bonhoeffer and Henri Nouwen emphasize the significance of mental health within Christian communities. Bonhoeffer's concept of "the ministry of bearing" encourages leaders to empathize with and support individuals struggling with mental health issues.

Contrary to common belief, historical texts have addressed and provided guidance on mental health. Unfortunately, this wisdom seems to have been overlooked in contemporary times. But from now on, we will not disregard this valuable insight.

Unique Challenges and Stressors Faced by Leaders

Leaders face unique spiritual challenges that arise from our calling to guide our congregations. These challenges take on various forms.

Challenge: Emotions. First, let's talk about Emotions. I know; we've been taught that strong men (or women) don't cry, i.e., show emotions. It's often viewed as a sign of weakness. Unfortunately, that misinterpretation has led to the demise of many leaders! Not acknowledging emotions doesn't make them go away. Leaders often face emotional challenges that can significantly impact their well-being, yet these challenges are frequently overlooked. We are expected to provide emotional support to our congregants while simultaneously dealing with our own emotional struggles. Scriptural references, such as Galatians 6:2 and 1 Thessalonians 5:11, emphasize the importance of mutual support and encouragement within the Christian community. Theologians like Henri Nouwen and Richard Foster shed light on the emotional toll leadership can take and the need for self-care and vulnerability.

Challenge: Stress and Burnout. Another hot topic is Stress and Burnout. These challenges include managing administrative tasks, financial responsibilities, and interpersonal conflicts within the congregation. I experienced this one firsthand. There was a season in my life when I was overwhelmed- caught in the whirlwind of responsibilities that came with teaching, preaching, and various other commitments. I believed that my dedication to my calling was noble, but as the weeks turned into months, I noticed the signs of burnout creeping in. My once-passionate spirit felt dulled, my energy was drained, and my ability to connect with others started to fade.

I realized that without a healthy balance, prioritizing Christ and operating in my true purpose, I was walking a tightrope that was bound to snap. It became clear that I needed to establish boundaries to protect my well-being. This is when I started to implement a mandatory Sabbath day. Given my teaching and preaching commitments, finding that time was tricky. I had no traditional weekends off, so I decided to designate Mondays as my day of rest. This simple but intentional choice made a profound difference in my life. It allowed me to step back, recharge, and reconnect with God and my own purpose.

Additionally, my wife and I recognized the importance of nurturing our relationship and family amidst our busy lives. We made a commitment to get away together every six months. Whether it's a weekend trip or a short escape, these moments became sacred—time to reconnect, reflect, and enjoy each other's company. During the summer, we extended this to two or three weeks of complete break, allowing us to rejuvenate and build lasting memories with our family.

These intentional practices have been transformative. They remind me that prioritizing my relationship with Christ and nurturing my marriage and family are essential to preventing burnout. It's a continual journey of learning and adjustment, but I've found that when I make space for rest and reflection, I can return to my purpose with renewed vigor and passion.

Through these experiences, I've come to appreciate the wisdom in setting aside time for rest. It's not merely a luxury; it's a necessity. By honoring that rhythm of rest and rejuvenation, I can better serve others and fulfill my calling without losing sight of what truly matters.

Challenge: Isolation. Apostolic leaders may experience feelings of loneliness and isolation due to the demands of our role. The prophet Elijah's experience in the wilderness (1 Kings 19:4-10) highlights the emotional struggles leaders face. Theologians stress the significance of building a support network to combat feelings of isolation.

Challenge: Warfare. Because our work brings advancement to God's Kingdom, Apostolic leaders have large targets on our backs! That is, we are often engaged in spiritual warfare, facing opposition and discouragement. The apostle Paul's letters reveal his battles with spiritual forces (Ephesians 6:12) and his moments of discouragement (2 Corinthians 1:8-9). Theologians emphasize the importance of spiritual disciplines, such as prayer and meditation, to strengthen apostolic leaders in their spiritual battles.

Undergoing these and other challenging experiences made me recognize the importance of mental health and became the impetus for building a framework that allows leaders to lead effectively, not from a place of exhaustion but from a place of emotional strength and wholeness.

Chapter 2- Self-Care

Self-care is not a luxury for leaders; it is a necessity. While serving others, we often neglect ourselves, leading to emotional depletion. This chapter focuses on the importance of self-care as a spiritual and emotional discipline. We will discuss practical strategies leaders can use to nurture our well-being, ensuring that we can continue serving with renewed energy and a sound mind. Self-care is the foundation for sustainable leadership.

The Bible emphasizes the importance of caring for our bodies, which are described as temples of the Holy Spirit (1 Corinthians 6:19-20). Neglecting our physical well-being can hinder our ability to serve God effectively. For instance, maintaining a balanced diet, engaging in regular exercise, and getting sufficient rest are all essential aspects of self-care that contribute to our overall well-being. By caring for our bodies, we honor God's creation and ensure we have the energy and vitality to fulfill our purpose.

We tend to get that part. Take care of the temple, right? Here's where the problem arises. **Self-care extends beyond physical health to encompass emotional and mental well-being**. The Bible encourages us to guard our hearts and minds (Proverbs 4:23, Philippians 4:6-7). Engaging in activities that promote emotional and mental well-being, such as practicing mindfulness, seeking counseling when needed, and cultivating healthy relationships,

Self-Care extends beyond physical health.

are all vital components of self-care. We can experience inner peace, resilience, and a deeper connection with God and others by prioritizing our emotional and mental health.

This is an area where I struggled! I couldn't win the battle on my own. It took me getting guidance from a trusted example… someone who had been in my shoes. Someone I could relate to, because he could relate to me. With this book, I'm extending that relativity to you!

Looking back on my experiences with my mentor, Dr. Dharius Daniels, I've realized the importance of maintaining good emotional and mental health as a leader. Having someone to guide and support us, along with prioritizing self-care and mental well-being, is crucial for effective leadership. Dr. Daniels provided practical suggestions to help me maintain good emotional and mental health. For instance, on Sundays, I pour out my heart, body, and soul as I minister as God's yielded vessel, giving my all to serve others. As a result, I've realized that I need to take it easy on Mondays after such an intense Sunday. I need to have some time for myself with no plans and focus on self-care. I need to refill, because I poured out so much. To neglect the refresh leaves me open to burnout. Many leaders are experts in caring for others while neglecting their own care.

That's another thing I'm working on- taking care of myself. I have made taking care of myself a priority. I wake up at 4 AM every day, stretch, and go to the gym on Monday, Wednesday, and Friday. Two years ago, my body was in bad shape from playing sports, and I never went to a chiropractor. I have come to realize that mental health and physical health go hand in hand. Taking care of our bodies is essential as everything is connected. If our body is in pain, it may lead to mental issues and vice versa. It's not an easy journey, but I believe it's crucial.

I've also learned the importance of being cautious about the advice I receive. You can't eat from everybody's table. Discernment is needed. But mental fatigue hinders your ability to discern wisely. It's crucial to be mindful of the information and advice we take in, as not everything offered to us is beneficial or reliable.

As a leader, I've come to realize the importance of maintaining a balanced lifestyle and knowing when to take breaks. Over time, I've learned the significance of taking mental breaks while working. It's essential for me to step away at regular intervals to clear my mind and free myself from work-related thoughts. Being a visionary, my mind is constantly active, so I need to create space for relaxation and detachment from work. I've made it a point to set boundaries, like not accepting work-related calls after 5 o'clock, not to be rude, but to ensure I have time to disconnect from work, even during sleep.

Here's an important caveat: as a conduit of God, we can disconnect from our natural work, but not from our spiritual connection. God never sleeps, so we must maintain mental margin to be ready to act when He speaks – even if it's 2 o'clock in the

We must maintain mental margin to be ready to act when He Speaks.

morning. Yes, you heard me right – 2 a.m. For example, last night, I woke up at 2 o'clock and received a revelation for our next series. When my wife asked me what I was doing, I told her that the Lord had just given me our next series. It was 2 in the morning, but that's how God operates.

At its core, self-care involves nurturing our spiritual well-being. Regular prayer, meditation, and studying the Scriptures are essential practices that help us grow spiritually and deepen our relationship with God. Jesus himself often withdrew to solitary places to pray and seek spiritual renewal (Luke 5:16). By setting aside time for spiritual nourishment, we can find solace, guidance, and strength in our faith, enabling us to face life's challenges with resilience and grace.

Here is another key distinction to make: Self-care and Selfishness are not synonyms, although many leaders have been made to feel that way, even if it is a subconscious association. Rather than a selfish pursuit, self-care is an essential aspect of living a life that honors God and fulfills our purpose. By incorporating self-care practices into our daily lives, we can experience holistic well-being and live in alignment with God's intentions for us. Let us remember that

Self-Care and Selfishness are not synonyms.

self-care is not a luxury but a responsibility, enabling us to love ourselves and others more fully.

The Role of Self-Care in Maintaining Mental Health-Scripture and Theologian Insights

As we strive to navigate the challenges of life, it becomes crucial to prioritize self-care practices that promote mental well-being. Scriptural references provide a foundation for understanding the importance of this prioritization. The Bible encourages individuals to prioritize self-care as an act of stewardship over their bodies and minds. For instance, 1 Corinthians 6:19-20 states, "Do you not know that your bodies are temples of the Holy Spirit, who is in you, whom you have received from God? You are not your own; you were bought at a price. Therefore, honor God with your bodies." This verse highlights the responsibility to care for our bodies, which includes mental well-being.

Theologians throughout history chimed in on this topic as well. St. Augustine, a prominent theologian, emphasized the importance of self-care as a means to cultivate a healthy soul. He believed that self-care practices, such as prayer, meditation, and reflection, were essential for nurturing one's mental and spiritual well-being. Similarly, Thomas Aquinas emphasized the importance of self-care in maintaining a balanced life, stating that self-care practices contribute to the overall flourishing of an individual.

Self-care practices encompass a wide range of activities that promote mental well-being. These practices can include physical exercise, adequate sleep, healthy eating, engaging in hobbies, spending time in nature, seeking therapy or counseling, and cultivating spiritual practices such as prayer and meditation. By practicing self-care, we can reduce stress, enhance emotional resilience, and foster a sense of inner peace.

The Role of Developing a Personalized Self-Care Plan

Let's move from theory to practice. An effective self-care plan must be holistic, nurturing our physical, emotional, and spiritual well-being. Developing a personalized plan aligns with biblical teachings, enabling us to live out our faith in a practical and tangible manner.

Addressing the Physical. A personalized self-care plan may include regular exercise, a balanced diet, and sufficient sleep. Prioritizing physical well-being can enhance energy levels, reduce stress, and improve overall health. Scriptural references such as 1 Corinthians 10:31 (*"So, whether you eat or drink, or* *whatever you do, do all to the glory of God*") remind us of the spiritual significance of caring for our bodies.

Addressing the Emotional. Emotional self-care involves recognizing and addressing our emotional needs. This may include seeking therapy, practicing mindfulness, or engaging in activities that bring joy and relaxation. The story of Jesus withdrawing to pray and find solace in times of emotional distress (Luke 5:16) serves as a powerful example of the importance of emotional self-care.

Addressing the Spiritual. Developing a personalized self-care plan should also encompass spiritual practices. This may involve regular prayer, meditation, or engaging with scripture. The example of Jesus retreating to the wilderness for forty days and nights to seek spiritual renewal (Matthew 4:1-11) highlights the significance of intentional spiritual self-care.

By prioritizing self-care, we honor God's creation, love others more fully, and embark on a journey of spiritual growth. Let us embrace the transformative power of self-care and embark on a path towards holistic well-being.

Exploring Practices of Mindfulness, Exercise, and Rest

Let's dig in a bit more. To begin with, **mindfulness,** rooted in ancient wisdom traditions, involves cultivating present-moment awareness and non-judgmental acceptance. Scriptural references, such as the Bhagavad Gita's teachings on self-awareness and the Bible's emphasis on being still and knowing God, highlight the importance of mindfulness in spiritual growth. Theologians like Thich Nhat Hanh and Eckhart Tolle have also emphasized the transformative potential of mindfulness in deepening our connection with the divine. For instance, practicing mindfulness meditation allows individuals to observe their thoughts and emotions without attachment, leading to a greater sense of inner peace and spiritual clarity.

Next, **physical exercise**, often overlooked in spiritual practices, plays a vital role in nurturing our spiritual well-being. Scriptural references, such as the Quran's emphasis on maintaining a healthy body and the Bible's recognition of the body as a temple, underscore the significance of physical well-being in spiritual growth. Theologians like St. Augustine and Thomas Aquinas have also acknowledged the interplay between physical and spiritual health. Engaging in regular exercise, whether through yoga, walking, or other forms of physical activity, not only enhances our physical vitality but also promotes mental clarity, emotional balance, and a deeper connection with the divine.

Finally, **rest**, often associated with physical rejuvenation, holds profound spiritual implications. Scriptural references, such as the Bible's teachings on the Sabbath and the Quran's emphasis on balance and moderation, highlight the importance of rest in spiritual growth. Theologians like Meister Eckhart and Thomas Merton have explored the transformative power of rest in contemplative practices. By allowing ourselves to rest, both physically and mentally, we create space for introspection, self-reflection, and communion with the divine. Restorative practices like meditation, prayer, and Sabbath observance enable us to recharge our spiritual batteries and cultivate a deeper sense of connection with the divine.

Incorporating mindfulness, exercise, and rest into our daily lives allows us to embark on a spiritual journey that transcends the boundaries of time and space. This journey leads us to a deeper understanding of ourselves and our connection with the divine.

Chapter 3- Emotional Intelligence & Social Awareness

Emotional intelligence is the foundation of effective leadership. It enables us to not only understand our own emotions but also navigate the emotions of those we lead. However, leadership also demands an acute social awareness—the ability to read the room, understand the dynamics at play, and respond with empathy and wisdom. Understanding how emotional intelligence and social awareness work hand-in-hand is important to create a balanced, effective leader. By cultivating these traits, leaders can foster deeper connections, reduce conflict, and lead with greater clarity and compassion, ultimately creating healthier environments for everyone.

This emotional insight helps leaders anticipate needs, diffuse tensions, and foster a supportive environment where individuals feel heard and valued. Socially aware leaders also excel in building deeper, more authentic relationships, which cultivate trust, loyalty, and collaboration. Without emotional intelligence, we may misinterpret our team's emotional state, overlook key issues, and struggle to motivate and inspire, ultimately weakening the bond between leader and team.

Emotional Intelligence and its Impact on Leadership

Before we unpack, let's define. Emotional intelligence (EI) encompasses the ability to recognize, understand, and manage one's own emotions effectively. Scripture provides numerous examples of individuals who demonstrated

Emotional Intelligence: The ability to recognize, understand, and manage one's own emotions effectively.

this, such as Jesus Christ. In the Gospel of Mark, Jesus displays emotional intelligence by expressing empathy towards the suffering of others, such as when he wept at the death of his friend Lazarus (John 11:35). This example highlights the importance of acknowledging and processing emotions, as well as the impact it can have on our interactions with others.

Social awareness involves perceiving and understanding the emotions and needs of those around us. Theologians have emphasized the significance of social awareness in fostering compassion and empathy. For instance, theologian Martin Buber emphasized the importance of the "I-Thou" relationship, which encourages individuals to genuinely engage with others and recognize their unique emotional experiences. By practicing social awareness, we can cultivate deeper connections and promote understanding within our communities.

> *Social Awareness: Perceiving and understanding the emotions and needs of those around us.*

Emotional intelligence and social awareness aren't just buzzwords; they are the invisible threads that hold our mental health together. Imagine navigating life without the ability to recognize your own feelings or understand the emotions of those around you—it would be like trying to steer a ship without a compass. As defined, emotional intelligence equips us with the ability to manage our emotions, while social awareness gives us the tools to connect and empathize with others. Together, they are vital for building healthy relationships, reducing stress, and fostering resilience. Without them, our mental and emotional well-being can unravel in isolation and misunderstanding. Without them, we can find ourselves in a perilous position for our own well-being and the health of those we lead.

Picture a leader who lacks the ability to recognize when stress is taking a toll on them. Unable to regulate their emotions, they might lash out at colleagues, make hasty decisions, or isolate themselves to avoid confrontation. Over time, this emotional disconnection breeds stress, burnout, and a sense of alienation—both personally and within the team.

Consider this real-life situation: Imagine a pastor leading a growing congregation. This pastor is passionate about their ministry but lacks emotional intelligence and social awareness. Over time, the pressures of counseling members, managing church operations, and delivering impactful sermons begin to take a toll. Because they are unaware of their own emotional state, they push through exhaustion, ignoring feelings of burnout. Their sermons become more robotic, and they grow increasingly irritable, misinterpreting others' concerns as personal attacks rather than cries for support.

One day, a long-time church member approaches the pastor after service, sharing that they feel distant from the church community and unsupported during a tough season. Without social awareness, the pastor, feeling overwhelmed and defensive, might respond dismissively, suggesting that the member "pray harder" or "trust God more." What the pastor misses is that the member is actually reaching out for emotional support and connection. This well-meaning but disconnected response leaves the member feeling hurt and misunderstood. They withdraw from the church, feeling as though the pastor doesn't care or understand their struggles. Sound familiar?

In contrast, a pastor with emotional intelligence and social awareness might pick up on the member's deeper emotional state—not just their words. He would recognize the unspoken feelings of loneliness or frustration and offer compassionate listening, validating the member's experience. By creating a space for honest dialogue, the pastor not only helps the individual but strengthens the overall sense of community.

Moreover, this emotionally intelligent pastor would also recognize when he becomes emotionally depleted. Rather than pushing through exhaustion, he might delegate responsibilities, take time to rest, or seek support from fellow leaders. This self-awareness allows him to serve his congregation more effectively without risking burnout or disconnecting from his own spiritual health.

Here is where many leaders get lost, and their mental health gets compromised. Without these skills, misunderstandings can lead to isolation, fractured relationships, and a sense of disconnection that undermines both the leader and the church.

Scripture and Theologian Insights-
Traits of an Emotionally Intelligent Leader

Self-Awareness. Emotional intelligence (EI) begins with self-awareness, the ability to recognize and understand one's own emotions. Scriptures such as Proverbs 16:32 emphasize the significance of self-control and self-discipline. By cultivating self-awareness, we can better manage our emotions, make rational decisions, and foster a positive environment. For instance, Mahatma Gandhi's ability to remain calm and composed during challenging times showcased his exceptional emotional intelligence, inspiring millions to follow his lead.

 Empathy. Effective leaders possess empathy - the capacity to understand and share the feelings of others. The Bible, in Matthew 7:12, encourages treating others as we would like to be treated, emphasizing the importance of empathy in building strong relationships. Leaders who demonstrate empathy create a supportive and inclusive work culture, fostering trust and collaboration. Nelson Mandela's ability to empathize with his oppressors and promote reconciliation in South Africa exemplifies the transformative power of empathy in leadership.

Social Awareness. Scriptural references, such as the Quran's emphasis on justice and compassion, highlight the significance of social awareness in leadership. Leaders who possess social awareness are attuned to the needs and concerns of their followers, promoting fairness and inclusivity. Theologian Martin Luther King Jr., through his powerful speeches and nonviolent activism, exemplified inspirational leadership rooted in social awareness. His ability to mobilize people toward a common goal while advocating for justice and equality showcased his exceptional emotional intelligence.

Self-awareness, empathy, and social awareness are key components of emotional intelligence that enable leaders to inspire and motivate others. By incorporating these principles into their leadership approach, we can cultivate emotional intelligence and create a positive impact on those we lead.

Developing Self-Awareness and Emotional Regulation Skills

Emotional regulation refers to the ability to manage and control one's emotions in a healthy and constructive manner. Self-awareness is the foundation upon which emotional regulation skills are built. By developing self-awareness, leaders can identify their emotions, triggers, and behavior patterns, enabling us to respond more effectively to challenging situations.

Emotional Regulation: The ability to manage and control one's emotions in a healthy and constructive manner.

Scriptural references emphasize the importance of introspection and self-reflection. For instance, the Bible encourages individuals to *"examine themselves"* (2 Corinthians 13:5) and "know *thyself"* (Proverbs 20:27). Theologians such as St. Augustine and Thomas Aquinas also emphasized self-knowledge as a means to spiritual growth.

In addition, scriptures highlight the importance of self-control and temperance in emotional regulation. For instance, the Bible advises individuals to *"be slow to anger"* (Proverbs 14:29) and *"put away all bitterness, wrath, and anger"* (Ephesians 4:31). Theologians such as St. Thomas Aquinas and St. John of the Cross also emphasized the need for emotional balance and moderation. By practicing emotional regulation, we can respond to emotional stimuli in a manner that aligns with our values and fosters positive relationships.

Chapter 4- Stress Management & Resilience

Leadership brings with it inevitable stress, but how we handle that stress determines the quality of our leadership. By learning to manage stress, we can prevent burnout and maintain our mental and emotional well-being. We will explore practical techniques that can be incorporated into daily life to help leaders not only cope with stress but thrive amid it.

First, to manage stress effectively, it is crucial to comprehend its origins and manifestations. Let's begin with a working definition. **Stress** is the body's physical and emotional response to external pressures or demands that disrupt an individual's

equilibrium, often resulting in feelings of
tension, anxiety, or overwhelm (American Psychological Association). Notable
scriptures shed light on the nature of
stress and recount numerous instances
where individuals faced overwhelming
stress, e.g. Job's trials or Jesus' agony in
the Garden of Gethsemane. These narratives provide examples of how stress can manifest in different forms and the
emotional toll it can take on individuals.

Stress:
The body's physical
and emotional re-
sponse to external
pressures.

Further, scriptures and theologians emphasize the role of faith
and spirituality in managing stress. For instance, theologian
Thomas Aquinas highlighted the importance of prayer and
contemplation as means to find solace and inner peace amidst
stressors. Similarly, Psalm 55:22 encourages individuals to cast
their burdens upon God, finding comfort and strength in their
faith. In addition, the Bible teaches us in Matthew 6:34, *"Therefore do not worry about tomorrow, for tomorrow will worry about itself.
Each day has enough trouble of its own."* This verse emphasizes the
importance of living in the moment and not allowing worries
about the future to consume us.

Let's continue with another definition. **Resilience** is the ability to bounce back from adversity and maintain a positive outlook despite challenging circumstances. (American Psychological Association). Scriptural references provide numerous examples of individuals who demonstrated resilience in the face of trials. Job's story in the Bible is a powerful illustration of resilience, as he endured immense suffering while remaining steadfast in his faith. Theologians such as Dietrich Bonhoeffer also offer insights into the importance of resilience, emphasizing that it is through adversity that our character is refined and strengthened. Now that we have working definitions and scriptural examples, let's move to the resolutions, which are how to manage stress and enable resilience.

Resilience: The ability to bounce back from adversity and maintain a positive outlook.

Techniques and Practical Strategies

Prayer, Meditation, and Counsel are powerful, practical strategies for recognizing and managing stress, especially for leaders. **Prayer** serves as a spiritual release, allowing leaders to express their concerns, frustrations, and fears to God. It is a space where we can find peace, gain clarity, and release the weight of our responsibilities.

Through **meditation**, we can quiet our minds, focus on the present, and cultivate mindfulness, which helps reduce anxiety and stress. Meditation allows us to pause in the midst of chaos, bringing emotional balance and mental clarity.

Counsel, whether through a trusted mentor, therapist, or spiritual advisor, offers a safe space to process thoughts and feelings. It provides a valuable external perspective, helping leaders identify sources of stress that may be overlooked and offering guidance on navigating them. Together, these practices foster emotional resilience, helping leaders stay grounded and better equipped to manage the pressures of our roles.

Keys to Building Resilience and Coping Strategies

As noted, resilience is essential for leaders to navigate stress and maintain effectiveness, but it doesn't develop overnight—it must be intentionally built. Key strategies for building resilience include cultivating Hope, Community, and Acceptance. **Hope** involves maintaining a positive outlook even in challenging circumstances. This can be achieved by setting small, achievable goals and celebrating progress along the way. Likewise, developing a strong sense of **Community** is equally Important. Leaders who surround themselves with supportive individuals—whether peers, mentors, or loved ones—are more likely to bounce back from setbacks. Community provides not only encouragement but also diverse perspectives and solutions to problems. Additionally, **Acceptance** is vital in building resilience. Leaders must accept that stress and difficulties are part of the journey and learn to embrace rather than resist them. This mindset allows for adaptability and growth.

Finally, **Coping Strategies** like mindfulness, journaling, and regular reflection can help leaders process their emotions and reduce stress. By focusing on these elements, we can build a resilient foundation that empowers us to endure and thrive through adversity.

Scripture and Theologian Insights

Now, let's see what the scriptures and theologians have to say on these topics.

Hope. Theologians, such as Saint Augustine, have emphasized the significance of hope in fostering resilience. Augustine's writings emphasize the importance of maintaining hope even in the darkest of times. We can find the strength to persevere and overcome challenges by cultivating a hopeful mindset. This notion is echoed in scriptural passages, such as Romans

12:12, which encourages believers to *"be joyful in hope, patient in affliction, faithful in prayer."*

Community. The Bible frequently emphasizes the power of unity and support to foster resilience within a community. Ecclesiastes 4:9-10 states, *"Two are better than one because they have a good return for their labor: If either of them falls down, one can help the other up."* This passage highlights the strength that can be derived from supportive relationships, which can provide solace, encouragement, and practical assistance during challenging times.

Acceptance. Theologians, such as Thomas Aquinas, have explored the concept of acceptance as a coping strategy. He argues that accepting the limitations of our human condition and surrendering to God's will can lead to inner peace and resilience. This perspective aligns with teachings, such as the Serenity Prayer, which encourages us to accept the things we cannot change and find the courage to change the things we can.

Mastering stress and resilience is the secret weapon of unstoppable leaders. It's not just about handling the heat; it's about transforming challenges into fuel for growth. When we learn to rise above the pressure, we don't just survive—we lead with boldness, inspire others, and turn every setback into a launchpad for greater impact.

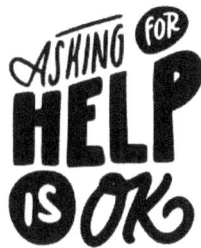

Chapter 5- Burnout Prevention & Recovery

Burnout is one of the most common threats to leaders, yet it is often overlooked until it's too late. In this chapter, we will examine the signs of burnout and discuss strategies for both preventing and recovering from it. By addressing burnout head-on, we can create sustainable practices that allow leaders to recover and return to their calling with renewed passion and purpose.

Signs of Burnout

Burnout in leadership often manifests through a combination of emotional, physical, and behavioral signs. Leaders experiencing burnout may feel constantly drained and emotionally exhausted, losing the passion or motivation that once fueled their work. They may become detached or cynical toward their responsibilities, colleagues, or organization, often leading to a sense of isolation or feeling disconnected from their purpose. Physical symptoms such as frequent headaches, sleep disturbances, and chronic fatigue may also occur, signaling that the body is under prolonged stress. Behavioral changes, like increased irritability, procrastination, or difficulty concentrating, are common as well. Leaders may also experience a decline in performance, struggling to make decisions or solve problems as effectively as before. Sound familiar? These signs, if left unaddressed, can escalate and severely impact both the individual leader and the organization they serve.

Burnout is not merely exhaustion or stress; it is a state of chronic physical, emotional, and mental exhaustion resulting from prolonged exposure to stressors. Scripture provides examples of individuals who experienced burnout, such as Elijah, who became overwhelmed and despondent after his encounter with the prophets of Baal (1 Kings 19:1-4). In Numbers 11:14-15, Moses reached a breaking point, saying to God, *"I cannot carry all these people by myself; the burden is too heavy for me. If this is how you are going to treat me, please go ahead and kill me."* Moses felt the weight of leadership so heavily that he despaired of continuing. It happened then; it happens now.

> *Burnout:*
> *The state of chronic physical, emotional, and mental exhaustion...from prolonged exposure to stressors.*

Strategies for Prevention

Preventing burnout requires intentional strategies that nurture both personal well-being and spiritual health. One key strategy is setting **clear boundaries** to protect time for rest and rejuvenation, ensuring that work doesn't consume every waking moment. Regularly scheduling downtime, exercise, and hobbies can help leaders recharge.

> *We don't have to carry every burden alone!*

Delegation is another critical tool—we don't have to carry every burden alone. Empowering others creates space for leaders to focus on their own well-being. Equally important is nurturing the **relationship with God**, which serves as a spiritual anchor. Through daily prayer, meditation on scripture, and moments of stillness, leaders can find peace, clarity, and renewed strength. By staying connected to God's guidance, we gain perspective and learn to trust that we are not leading in our own power but through divine wisdom. Regularly participating in a **spiritual community**, such as church or small groups, can also provide encouragement and accountability, helping leaders avoid isolation and stay spiritually refreshed.

The story of Daniel (Daniel 6:10) illustrates how this leader utilized consistent prayer and devotion as a preventive measure against spiritual brownouts. Theologian Thomas Aquinas emphasizes the significance of cultivating virtues and engaging in spiritual disciplines to safeguard against spiritual depletion.

Strategies for Recovery

Recovering from burnout requires a multifaceted approach that addresses both the mind and body. The first step is to **acknowledge the burnout** and give yourself permission to rest. Taking time away from leadership responsibilities, even briefly, allows the mind and body to heal from prolonged stress. **Re-establishing self-care routines**—like consistent sleep, balanced nutrition, exercise, and relaxation—helps restore energy levels. Another key strategy is seeking **professional support**, such as counseling or coaching, which provides guidance in processing emotions and rebuilding mental resilience. **Spiritual rejuvenation** is also essential; reconnecting with God through prayer, reflection, or quiet moments in His presence can bring emotional renewal and peace. Leaders should also lean into our **support system**—whether through family, friends, or a faith community—allowing others to pour into us during recovery. Lastly, redefining personal and professional **boundaries** is crucial, ensuring that balance is maintained moving forward to prevent a recurrence of burnout.

The story of the prodigal son's return (Luke 15:11-32) beautifully illustrates the power of repentance in burnout recovery. After squandering his inheritance and reaching rock bottom, the son found himself physically and emotionally exhausted, feeding pigs and longing for their food. Recognizing his mistakes, he humbly decided to return to his father, acknowledging his wrongdoing. His father, filled with compassion, welcomed him with open arms, offering forgiveness and restoration. This story parallels the journey of leaders recovering from burnout: repentance, self-reflection, and a return to God's grace lead to healing, renewal, and a restored sense of purpose.

The theologian John Wesley emphasizes that personal reflection, confession, and seeking spiritual guidance are essential components in the journey toward recovery, especially for those in leadership. Wesley believed that spiritual healing begins with honest self-reflection—taking time to examine one's heart, motives, and relationship with God. Confession, both to God and within a trusted community, serves as a powerful act of humility and accountability, helping to release the weight of guilt, shame, or unresolved burdens. Wesley also stressed the importance of seeking spiritual guidance from mentors or spiritual advisors, as they can offer wisdom, support, and clarity during times of struggle. By embracing these practices, leaders can find not only recovery from burnout but also deeper spiritual renewal and growth.

Burnout is not the end of the road, but a wake-up call—a reminder that we are human, not invincible. It's an invitation to pause, reassess, and realign our lives with what truly matters. By taking time to focus on our mental health and well-being, we not only recover but emerge stronger, wiser, and more equipped to lead with purpose and passion.

BREAK
• the •
STIGMA

Chapter 6- Stigma & Seeking Help

For as long as I can remember, leaders have been expected to be invincible. Whether in the church, the boardroom, or the political arena, the mantle of leadership often comes with an unspoken rule: never show weakness. As a leader, I've felt the weight of this expectation. There's an unrelenting pressure to have all the answers, to carry the burdens of others, and to present a calm, composed exterior even when storms are raging within.

But what happens when the pressure becomes too much? When the demands of leadership begin to crack the very foundation of our mental and emotional well-being? I've seen it happen to those I admire—leaders who seemed unshakable, yet behind the scenes, were battling anxiety, depression, and burnout in silence. For some, the weight became unbearable. There is a deep-rooted stigma that keeps leaders from seeking help. **It's the fear of being judged, of being seen as incapable or weak, and of losing the trust of those who look up to us.** In a world that glorifies strength and resilience, admitting that we're struggling feels like failure. But that couldn't be further from the truth.

I write this not just as a call for compassion but as a personal plea for courage. Leaders need help, too! We are not immune to the toll that mental health challenges can take, and it's time we shed the stigma surrounding seeking support. It's time we embrace the truth that **vulnerability is not weakness...it's strength.**

This conversation is long overdue. It's an invitation for every leader, whether standing at the pulpit or sitting in the corner office, to step out of the shadows and embrace the help we all deserve. Because leadership isn't about being invincible; it's about being human.

This conversation is long OVERDUE!

This chapter breaks down the stigma and encourages leaders to seek the help they need. We will discuss how vulnerability is a strength and how seeking mental health support can actually enhance leadership, not diminish it. Breaking the silence is the first step toward healing!

Breaking the Silence

Breaking the silence around seeking help is crucial for leaders because it shatters the myth that strength means never struggling. When leaders openly acknowledge their need for support, they not only free themselves from the isolation and pressure to appear invincible but also create a healthier culture for those they lead. By normalizing vulnerability, leaders demonstrate that it's okay to seek help, paving the way for others to do the same without fear of judgment.

Vulnerability is a Strength

Vulnerability, far from being a weakness, is a strength that deepens a leader's authenticity and relatability. When leaders admit they don't have all the answers, it fosters trust and connection with their teams. This transparency allows leaders to lead more empathetically and with greater emotional intelligence, strengthening their relationships and influence. Seeking mental health support, whether through counseling, therapy, or mentorship, equips leaders with the tools to manage stress, maintain clarity, and make better decisions. In the end, it enhances their capacity to lead effectively, ensuring they can serve with longevity, resilience, and wisdom.

The Importance of Community

What happens when the weight of leadership becomes overwhelming? When the very people who depend on us don't realize that we, too, are struggling? It's in these moments that having a trusted community is not just important; it's vital. Leaders need a space where they can be vulnerable, where they don't have to pretend they have all the answers, and where authenticity is not just welcomed but encouraged.

I've learned firsthand how isolating leadership can be when you feel you must carry your burdens alone. It's exhausting, and the emotional toll can be immense. But when you find a community where you can be poured into—where others can offer you the support, love, and understanding you need—it becomes a lifeline. It's in these safe spaces that leaders can release their frustrations, process their pain, and be reminded that they are human, too. We weren't meant to lead from a place of emptiness, and without a community to hold us up, the journey becomes far harder than it needs to be. Leadership is not a solo journey, and finding a community to walk alongside us can make all the difference.

Addressing Mental Health Stigma in Leadership

To effectively address mental health stigma, leaders must first comprehend its nature and impact. By examining scriptural references, such as the Bible's teachings on compassion and empathy, leaders can gain a deeper understanding of the importance of supporting individuals struggling with mental health issues. For instance, the parable of the Good Samaritan (Luke 10:25-37) emphasizes the need for leaders to show kindness and care towards those in distress, including those facing mental health challenges.

 Leaders play a crucial role in challenging stigmatizing beliefs and attitudes towards mental health. Leaders can actively combat mental health stigma by drawing upon the insights of renowned theologians, such as Dietrich Bonhoeffer, who emphasized the importance of embracing the "other" and rejecting societal prejudices. Bonhoeffer's writings on the concept of "otherness" can inspire leaders to foster an environment of acceptance and understanding where individuals with mental health issues are treated with dignity and respect.

These scriptural references highlight the need to overcome the stigma and shame associated with seeking help.

James 5:16 (NIV): *"Therefore confess your sins to each other and pray for each other so that you may be healed. The prayer of a righteous person is powerful and effective."* This verse encourages mutual vulnerability, confession, and prayer, emphasizing that healing—both physical and emotional—comes through community and openness.

Proverbs 11:14 (ESV): *"Where there is no guidance, a people falls, but in an abundance of counselors there is safety."* This passage underscores the wisdom and strength in seeking counsel and guidance from others, dispelling the myth that leaders must handle their challenges alone.

Galatians 6:2 (NIV): *"Carry each other's burdens, and in this way you will fulfill the law of Christ."* Leaders are called not to bear their burdens in isolation but to share them with others, demonstrating the importance of mutual support and humility in seeking help.

By recognizing that everyone faces challenges and that seeking assistance is a sign of strength, we can create an environment where leaders feel empowered to reach out for support without fear of judgment or condemnation.

Understanding the Role of Therapy and Counseling: A Scriptural and Theological Perspective

Multiple scriptural references emphasize the significance of mental health and well-being. For instance, in the New Testament, Jesus encourages his followers to love their neighbors as themselves (Mark 12:31). This commandment implies the need for self-care and self-compassion, which includes attending to one's mental health. By acknowledging the importance of mental well-being, scripture lays the foundation for integrating therapy and counseling into religious practices.

Therapy and counseling can serve as tools for spiritual growth and self-reflection. The therapy process often involves exploring one's thoughts, emotions, and behaviors, which aligns with the concept of self-examination found in many religious traditions. By addressing underlying psychological issues, we can remove barriers that hinder our spiritual development, leading to a deeper connection with their faith and a stronger relationship with God.

Prominent theologians have also recognized the value of therapy and counseling within a religious framework. For example, St. Augustine emphasized the importance of seeking guidance from others to overcome personal struggles. Similarly, theologian Thomas Aquinas argued that therapy and counseling can aid individuals in achieving moral and spiritual growth. These theological perspectives support the integration of therapy and counseling into religious practices, highlighting their potential to enhance one's spiritual journey.

For the sake of your well-being, your calling, and those you lead, I urge you to set aside the stigma and shame—embrace the courage to seek the help you need, knowing that true strength lies in acknowledging our humanity and trusting God to walk with us through the healing process.

Chapter 7- Spiritual Well-Being

How are mental health and spiritual well-being interconnected? How can nurturing one's spiritual life enhance emotional and mental well-being? How can spiritual practices such as prayer, meditation, and reflection bring clarity and peace to leaders? In what ways does a healthy spiritual life create a solid foundation for emotional resilience for leaders? Let's explore the answers to these questions and more.

Interconnection: Mental Health and Spiritual Well-Being

Let's begin by exploring the intersection of spirituality and mental health. Spirituality, often rooted in religious beliefs and practices, has long been recognized as a source of comfort, hope, and meaning for individuals facing mental health challenges. Numerous studies have shown that individuals who engage in spiritual practices, such as prayer, meditation, and attending religious services, experience lower levels of stress, anxiety, and depression. Scriptural references, such as the Psalms, highlight the power of spirituality in providing solace and strength during times of distress.

Moreover, spirituality can serve as a coping mechanism in adversity, providing leaders with a sense of purpose, resilience, and social support. The teachings of theologians, such as Thomas Aquinas and St. Augustine, emphasize the importance of spirituality in navigating life's challenges. By turning to their faith, we can find comfort, guidance, and a sense of belonging, which can positively impact our mental well-being.

Nurturing Spiritual Life for Emotional Well-being

Nurturing one's spiritual life is essential for enhancing emotional and mental well-being, especially for leaders constantly giving of themselves. When a leader's spiritual life is strong, they have a wellspring of peace, strength, and resilience to draw from.

> *A strong spiritual life brings a wellspring of peace, strength, and resilience.*

Spiritual practices like prayer, meditation, and scripture study help leaders process their emotions, calm their minds, and find grounding amidst the pressures they face. This soul nurturing brings a deep sense of inner peace, even in challenging times, positively affecting emotional stability and mental clarity.

For example, Philippians 4:6-7 reminds us: *"Do not be anxious about anything, but in every situation, by prayer and petition, with thanksgiving, present your requests to God. And the peace of God, which transcends all understanding, will guard your hearts and your minds in Christ Jesus."* This scripture speaks directly to the connection between spiritual practices and emotional well-being. When we take time to bring our worries and challenges before God in prayer, we receive His peace, a peace that protects both our hearts and minds from becoming overwhelmed by anxiety or stress. This divine peace allows leaders to lead with clarity and compassion, even in the face of difficult circumstances.

Similarly, the theologian St. Augustine illustrated how nurturing one's spiritual life can bring mental and emotional relief. In his *Confessions,* Augustine describes his personal journey of seeking peace and fulfillment through worldly pursuits, only to find lasting peace when he turned to God. He famously said, *"You have made us for yourself, O Lord, and our hearts are restless until they rest in you."* This statement encapsulates the transformative power of a healthy spiritual life—when we root ourselves in God, our restlessness, anxiety, and emotional turmoil begin to settle. Augustine's experience shows that true emotional and mental well-being comes not from external achievements or success, but from an intimate relationship with God.

When we invest in our spiritual life, we experience a greater sense of purpose and direction, which enhances our emotional resilience and mental health. In times of difficulty, nurturing our own relationship with God offers us a safe place to process feelings, find peace, and regain focus. This spiritual grounding enables leaders to navigate challenges gracefully, leading from a place of wholeness and inner strength, rather than depletion or emotional fatigue.

How Spiritual Practices Bring Mental Clarity to Leaders

Spiritual practices such as prayer, meditation, and reflection are powerful tools for leaders seeking clarity and peace in their lives. These practices allow leaders to pause amidst leadership demands, offering space to reconnect with their purpose, align with their values, and gain a fresh perspective. When a leader is constantly on the move, making decisions and responding to the needs of others, it can be easy to lose sight of their inner compass. Spiritual practices serve as an anchor, helping leaders ground themselves and listen for divine guidance.

For example, consider a pastor who leads a growing congregation. As the church expands, so do the pressures and responsibilities. The pastor gets caught in the whirlwind of meetings, counseling sessions, and sermon preparation, often feeling overwhelmed by the needs of the community. To manage everything, he starts to lose sight of his own emotional and spiritual health, becoming frustrated and disconnected.

One morning, realizing that the frustration is impacting his ability to lead effectively, the pastor dedicates time to prayer and reflection. He sits in silence, allowing his heart to quiet down and his mind to release the pressures of the day. In prayer, he seeks guidance, asking for wisdom and peace. As he reflects on the previous week, he recognizes areas where he's been stretched too thin and where relationship tension has built up too much.

Through this practice of prayer and meditation, the pastor gains clarity on a decision he's been wrestling with—whether to delegate certain responsibilities to trusted leaders within the church. This spiritual moment reveals that it's not only acceptable but necessary to release control in certain areas, allowing others to step up. In turn, this brings a sense of peace, knowing that his calling is not about doing everything alone but trusting God's provision through others.

This experience of clarity through prayer doesn't just solve one problem; it restores the pastor's sense of purpose and confidence. He emerges with a refreshed mindset, better equipped to lead with a peaceful heart, and more conscious of his boundaries and responsibilities. By integrating spiritual practices into his daily routine, the pastor cultivates ongoing clarity and peace, preventing burnout and maintaining a healthy balance in his leadership. Spiritual practices remind us to look inward and upward, allowing us to lead from a place of wholeness and divine alignment.

How a Healthy Spiritual Life Supports Resilience

A healthy spiritual life provides leaders with a solid foundation for emotional resilience by offering a consistent source of strength, peace, and perspective. When deeply rooted in our spiritual life, we are better equipped to handle challenges, disappointments, and stress calmly and purposefully. Spiritual practices such as prayer, reflection, and scripture meditation help leaders remain grounded, especially when circumstances feel overwhelming. This inner strength acts as a buffer against emotional fatigue and burnout, allowing us to continue serving without losing sight of our core values and calling.

Consider the biblical reference from Isaiah 40:31: *"But those who wait on the Lord shall renew their strength; they shall mount up with wings like eagles, they shall run and not be weary, they shall walk and not faint."* This verse perfectly captures the relationship between spiritual life and emotional resilience. Leaders who consistently seek God's presence—who "wait on the Lord"—find our strength renewed. We are empowered to face our responsibilities and challenges without growing weary. Spiritual nourishment from God replenishes our emotional reserves, enabling us to rise above difficulties like an eagle soaring above a storm. This resilience is not a result of our own effort, but a divine strength that sustains us in difficult times.

A healthy spiritual life also provides perspective in moments of frustration or emotional strain. When we are connected to God through prayer and meditation, we are reminded of the bigger picture. We can rise above immediate pressures and find peace in knowing we are not navigating life alone. This gives us the emotional flexibility to adapt to change and endure hardships without becoming overwhelmed.

For example, a ministry leader might face constant criticism, conflicting demands, or personal struggles that threaten to derail his sense of purpose. But with a solid spiritual foundation, we can draw from the well of God's wisdom and comfort, allowing us to process these emotions healthily rather than reacting impulsively. Through daily spiritual disciplines, we maintain the clarity to lead with grace under pressure and respond to challenges with patience and understanding.

With a solid spiritual foundation, we can draw from the well of God's Wisdom.

Ultimately, a healthy spiritual life instills leaders with emotional resilience by constantly reminding us of our source of strength, our purpose, and the assurance that we are being guided by something greater than ourselves

Chapter 8- Boundaries & Healthy Relationships

Setting boundaries is crucial for protecting a leader's mental and emotional health. Without boundaries, leaders can become overwhelmed, leading to burnout, frustration, and strained relationships. In this chapter, we will explore how leaders can establish healthy boundaries in both their personal and professional lives, while also navigating difficult relationships and conflicts that may arise. Healthy relationships—whether with colleagues, family, or congregants—are essential for sustaining leadership. By learning to set boundaries and hold themselves accountable, leaders can foster connections that are supportive, respectful of their well-being, and grounded in mutual trust and integrity.

Boundaries and Healthy Relationships for Leaders

Leaders who lack clear boundaries often find themselves over-whelmed, emotionally drained, and unable to lead effectively. The renowned theologian Henri Nouwen reflects on the dangers of boundarylessness, stating, "Without solitude, it is virtually impossible to live a spiritual life" (Nouwen, 1975). By setting boundaries, leaders create space for self-care, reflection, and rejuvenation, ultimately enhancing their emotional well-being and capacity for effective leadership.

Scripture also provides a foundation for understanding the significance of boundaries in relationships. In the book of Proverbs, we find the wisdom of King Solomon, who emphasizes the importance of guarding one's heart (Proverbs 4:23). This verse highlights the need for personal boundaries, as leaders must protect their emotional well-being and maintain a healthy inner life. Additionally, the apostle Paul encourages believers to *"speak the truth in love"* (Ephesians 4:15), emphasizing the importance of setting boundaries through honest and compassionate communication.

.

Theologian and psychologist Dr. Henry Cloud emphasizes that boundaries define where one person ends and another begins.[5] By setting clear boundaries, leaders can foster respect, trust, and mutual understanding within their relationships. Boundaries also enable leaders to establish healthy limits, preventing the exploitation of their time, energy, and resources.

Establishing Healthy Boundaries in Personal and Professional Lives

Establishing healthy boundaries is essential for leaders to maintain their well-being and effectiveness. Without clear boundaries, leaders risk burnout, emotional fatigue, and diminished impact. Here are key ways to create and maintain healthy boundaries in both personal and professional life:

1. **Define Non-Negotiables**: Leaders must identify what's most important—such as family time, personal self-care, or key professional priorities—and protect these areas.

2. **Set Limits on Availability**: Leaders should establish clear work hours and communication windows, limiting work-related tasks during personal time to maintain balance.

3. **Delegate Responsibilities**: Effective leaders delegate tasks to empower others and avoid overloading themselves with unnecessary duties.

4. **Learn to Say No**: Saying no to additional commitments helps leaders focus on their priorities and prevents them from being stretched too thin.

5. **Prioritize Self-Care**: Leaders must schedule regular self-care activities, whether through exercise, rest, or spiritual practices, to stay emotionally and physically strong.

By implementing these boundaries, we protect our energy, ensure long-term success, and set an example for those we lead.

Navigating Difficult Relationships and Conflicts

Navigating difficult relationships and conflicts is an inevitable part of leadership, but how a leader approaches these challenges can define the health and harmony of their environment. Traits like love, compassion, forgiveness, and humility are not just ideals—they are vital tools that allow leaders to resolve conflicts with grace and maintain strong, authentic relationships. These qualities help leaders respond to challenges with

Conflict is an inevitable part of leadership.

empathy, foster reconciliation, and create a culture of mutual respect. By leading with love and humility, we can turn conflict into an opportunity for growth and deeper connection.

"Above all, love each other deeply, because love covers over a multitude of sins." (1 Peter 4:8). Love and compassion lie at the heart of navigating difficult relationships and conflicts. The Bible teaches us that love has the power to heal wounds, bridge gaps, and transform hearts. By approaching challenging relationships with a deep sense of love and compassion, we can create an environment conducive to reconciliation and growth.

In the parable of the prodigal son (Luke 15:11-32), Jesus illustrates the power of love and compassion. Despite his son's rebellion and waywardness, the father welcomes him back with open arms, demonstrating unconditional love and forgiveness. This story reminds us of the transformative power of love in healing broken relationships.

"Bear with each other and forgive one another if any of you has a grievance against someone. Forgive as the Lord forgave you." (Colossians 3:13). Forgiveness is a crucial aspect of navigating difficult relationships and conflicts. It frees us from the burden of resentment and allows for healing and reconciliation. The Bible teaches us

to forgive others as we have been forgiven by God, emphasizing the transformative power of forgiveness.

Jesus exemplified forgiveness on the cross when he prayed, *"Father, forgive them, for they do not know what they are doing"* (Luke 23:34). Despite the immense pain and injustice He faced, Jesus chose to forgive his persecutors, setting an example for us to follow in our own relationships.

"Let your conversation be always full of grace, seasoned with salt, so that you may know how to answer everyone." (Colossians 4:6). Effective communication and humility play a vital role in navigating difficult relationships and conflicts. The Bible encourages us to approach conversations gracefully, seeking understanding and resolution rather than escalating tensions. Humility allows us to acknowledge our own faults and shortcomings, fostering an environment of mutual respect and empathy.

In the book of James, we are reminded of the power of humility in resolving conflicts. James 4:6 states, *"God opposes the proud but shows favor to the humble."* By humbling ourselves and seeking reconciliation, we open the door to healing and restoration in our relationships.

James 1:5 continues by saying, *"If any of you lacks wisdom, you should ask God, who gives generously to all without finding fault, and it will be given to you."* Navigating difficult relationships and conflicts requires wisdom and discernment. The Bible encourages us to seek guidance from God, who is the ultimate source of wisdom. By seeking divine wisdom, we can gain clarity to navigate challenging situations with grace and understanding.

In the book of Proverbs, wisdom is personified as a valuable companion who offers guidance in all aspects of life. Proverbs 2:6-7 states, *"For the Lord gives wisdom; from his mouth come knowledge and understanding. He holds success in store for the upright. He is a shield to those whose walk is blameless."* By seeking wisdom from God, we can navigate difficult relationships and conflicts with discernment and grace.

Finally, scriptural references provide timeless wisdom and guidance for navigating difficult relationships and conflicts. By embracing love and compassion, practicing forgiveness, engaging in effective communication and humility, and seeking divine wisdom, we can foster healthy relationships and resolve conflicts in a constructive manner. As believers, let us turn to the scriptures as a source of inspiration and guidance, allowing their teachings to shape our interactions and promote harmony in our relationships.

Accountability for Mental Health in Ministry

Accountability is a biblical principle that provides a framework for personal growth and maintaining mental health. Proverbs 27:17 states, *"As iron sharpens iron, so one person sharpens another."* Just as iron sharpening iron requires friction, accountability involves challenging and edifying one another. Leaders in ministry should actively seek accountability partners who can provide

Iron sharpens Iron!

guidance, correction, and support. By allowing others to hold them accountable, leaders can address potential blind spots, prevent burnout, and maintain a healthy perspective on their mental well-being.

As a passionate leader in ministry, I've always felt an unwavering drive to fulfill God's call on my life. I remember a particularly busy season when our church was preparing for a major outreach event. I was excited, fueled by purpose, and determined to make it a success. I dove headfirst into planning, coordinating teams, and ensuring every detail was perfect.

In the midst of the whirlwind, I felt like I was on a mission, pushing through fatigue and stress with the mindset that I had to keep going—for the sake of my congregation, for the sake

69

of the calling. However, as the days turned into weeks, I started to notice subtle changes within me. I became irritable and easily frustrated, and my usual joy in serving began to wane. It was as if I was running on fumes, yet I was conditioned to ignore the warning signs.

One evening, after a long day of meetings and preparations, I sat alone in my office, looking at my to-do list, which seemed to grow longer rather than shorter. As I stared at the overwhelming tasks, I felt a wave of anxiety wash over me. That's when it hit me—I had neglected my own emotional and mental well-being in the pursuit of fulfilling my purpose. I was so busy pouring out to others that I had forgotten to refill my cup.

It was during that pivotal moment that I realized the importance of accountability in managing my mental health. I reached out to a trusted friend who happened to be a Coach. In our conversation, I expressed my struggles and the pressures I felt from both inside and outside the ministry. My Coach helped me understand that it was okay to step back, reset, and prioritize my mental health without guilt.

We talked about practical strategies for maintaining balance: setting boundaries around my time, the importance of self-care, and the power of simply saying "no" when necessary. I also found value in having a coach who could provide guidance and encouragement, reminding me that seeking help is not a sign of weakness but a step towards strength and resilience.

I came to understand that mental health in ministry isn't just about identifying spiritual warfare or demonic influences; sometimes, it's about recognizing our human limits and the need for support. Embracing coaching helped me develop healthier patterns, allowing me to serve from a place of abundance rather than depletion.

Today, I'm committed to accountability not just for myself but for those I lead. I encourage open conversations about mental health within our ministry, reminding others that taking care of ourselves is essential for effectively serving others. After all, we cannot pour from an empty cup, and it's okay to seek help on the journey

Chapter 9- Trauma-Informed Care

Many leaders carry the weight of past traumas that continue to influence their mental health and leadership style. This chapter will explore how trauma affects leaders, highlighting the importance of healing and supporting others who may also be experiencing trauma. We will begin by discussing *Understanding the Impact of Trauma on Mental Health in Ministry* and examining how unresolved trauma can shape leaders' emotional responses and decisions. Next, we will look at *Implementing Trauma-Informed Practices in Ministry Leadership Roles*, providing practical strategies for leading with empathy and awareness. Finally, we'll focus on *Creating Safe and Supportive Environments for Healing in Ministry*, offering insights on how leaders can foster emotionally safe spaces where both they and those they serve can experience healing and growth.

Understanding the Impact of Trauma on Mental Health

Before delving into the specifics of trauma-informed care, it is essential to first understand what trauma is and how it can impact individuals. Trauma is defined as an emotional response to a distressing or disturbing event that overwhelms an individual's ability to cope. Trauma can result from a wide range of experiences, including physical or emotional abuse, neglect, loss, or violence. The impact of trauma can be profound and long-lasting, affecting individuals' mental, emotional, and physical health.

> *Trauma: An emotional response to a distressing or disturbing event.*

Ministry work can be both rewarding and challenging. Those who serve in ministry often find themselves in positions where they are providing support and guidance to others during times of crisis and difficulty. This can take a toll on their own mental health, especially when they are exposed to trauma on a regular basis. Understanding the impact of trauma on mental health is crucial for those who work in this field to ensure they can continue providing effective care to others.

Trauma can manifest in a variety of ways, including anxiety, depression, and post-traumatic stress disorder. Those who work in ministry may experience these symptoms as a result of exposure to traumatic events in their work. Individuals in ministry need to recognize these signs and seek help when needed.

Trauma can significantly affect the brain, impacting cognitive function and emotional regulation, which can directly influence how a leader operates in ministry. Leaders dealing with unresolved trauma may struggle with decision-making, memory, or focus, leading to difficulty managing day-to-day tasks or long-term planning. Emotionally, they may be more reactive or sensitive to stress, causing heightened anxiety, irritability, or emotional exhaustion. This can manifest in conflict avoidance, difficulty handling criticism, or becoming overly controlling as a way to regain a sense of safety. In a ministry context, these challenges can hinder effective leadership, making it harder to build trust, lead with clarity, and foster a healthy, supportive environment for their congregation.

A minister who has been exposed to multiple traumatic events in their work may begin to experience symptoms of anxiety and depression. By recognizing these signs and seeking help from a mental health professional, they can receive the support they need to cope with the trauma they have experienced.

For example, a chaplain who works in a hospital may witness traumatic events regularly, such as the death of a patient. This can take a toll on their mental health, leading to symptoms of post-traumatic stress disorder. By practicing self-care techniques and seeking support from their colleagues, they can better cope with the trauma they are exposed to in their work.

Understanding the impact of trauma on mental health in ministry is crucial for those who work in this field. By recognizing the signs and symptoms of trauma, understanding how trauma affects the brain, and developing coping strategies, individuals in ministry can better care for themselves and continue to serve others effectively. It is important for those in ministry to prioritize their own mental health in order to continue providing support and guidance to those in need.

Implementing Trauma-Informed Practices in Ministry Leadership Roles

In recent years, there has been a growing recognition of the impact of trauma on individuals' mental health and well-being. As such, there has been an increased emphasis on implementing trauma-informed practices in various settings, including ministry leadership roles. In the context of ministry leadership roles, it is important to recognize that many individuals who seek support from religious or spiritual leaders may have experienced trauma in their lives. As such, ministry leaders must be equipped with the knowledge and skills to provide trauma-informed care to those in need. Incorporating trauma-informed practices in ministry leadership is essential for creating a supportive and healing environment for both leaders and congregants. Understanding the prevalence of trauma and its impact on individuals allows leaders to approach their roles with greater empathy and awareness. Here are some practical strategies to implement these practices effectively:

1. Foster a Safe and Supportive Environment:

Creating a safe space begins with building trust. Leaders should prioritize open communication, encouraging congregants to share their experiences without fear of judgment. Establishing clear boundaries and maintaining confidentiality reinforces a sense of security. Consider incorporating trauma-informed language in all communications, emphasizing compassion and understanding.

2. Educate and Train Staff:

Provide training on trauma-informed care for all ministry staff and volunteers. This education should cover the effects of trauma, how to recognize signs of distress, and ways to respond effectively. Understanding that behaviors often stem from trauma can help leaders approach situations with greater patience and compassion.

3. Practice Active Listening:

Empathetic listening is crucial for supporting those who have experienced trauma. Leaders should engage in active listening by giving their full attention, validating feelings, and avoiding interruptive responses. Leaders can foster healing and connection by creating an atmosphere where individuals feel heard and understood.

4. Incorporate Mindfulness and Self-Care:

Encourage leaders and congregants to practice mindfulness and self-care as a way to manage stress and emotional responses. Incorporating regular opportunities for prayer, meditation, or quiet reflection can help individuals ground themselves and find peace amidst challenges.

5. Be Aware of Triggers:

Leaders should be mindful of potential triggers that may arise in worship services or ministry activities. This awareness can guide the selection of songs, sermons, and discussions, ensuring that they are sensitive to the experiences of those who may have endured trauma.

6. Encourage Connection and Community:

Building a strong sense of community is vital in supporting those who have experienced trauma. Leaders should facilitate opportunities for congregants to connect with one another, whether through small groups, support circles, or shared service projects. These connections can create a network of support that promotes healing

7. Model Vulnerability:

By being open about their own struggles and the importance of seeking help, leaders can model vulnerability. This not only humanizes them but also encourages others to share their own experiences and seek support.

Additionally, ministry leaders can work to build partnerships with mental health professionals and other community resources to provide comprehensive support to individuals in need. By collaborating with other professionals and organizations, we can ensure that individuals receive the holistic care they need to address their trauma and work toward healing.

By understanding the impact of trauma, recognizing the benefits of trauma-informed care, and implementing key strategies for incorporating trauma-informed practices, we can create a safe and supportive environment for individuals to heal and thrive. Through a commitment to trauma-informed care, we can make a meaningful difference in the lives of those we serve.

Creating Safe and Supportive Environments for Healing in Ministry

At its core, trauma-informed care's ultimate goal is healing. We must create safe and supportive environments where individuals feel heard, understood, and empowered to effectively support them in their healing journey

Ministry is often a place where individuals turn to for solace, guidance, and support during times of crisis, trauma, or emotional distress. As such, it is crucial for leaders to create safe and supportive environments where individuals feel comfortable sharing their experiences, expressing their emotions, and seeking help. Safe and supportive environments in ministry can help individuals feel validated, understood, and accepted in their struggles, leading to a sense of healing and empowerment.

In the context of ministry, creating safe and supportive environments involves providing physical safety, emotional support, and spiritual guidance to individuals in need. **Physical safety** ensures that individuals feel secure and protected within the ministry setting, while **emotional support** involves offering empathy, compassion, and non-judgmental listening to individuals who are going through difficult times. **Spiritual guidance** can provide individuals with a sense of hope, purpose, and meaning in the midst of their struggles, helping them navigate their healing journey with faith and resilience.

Creating this safe space does not come without its unique challenges. On one hand, ministry settings can be deeply rooted in tradition, hierarchy, and religious doctrine, which may pose challenges in providing a safe and inclusive space for individuals with diverse backgrounds and experiences. Leaders may also face resistance or skepticism from congregants who are not accustomed to discussing trauma, mental health, or emotional struggles within a religious context.

However, leaders also have unique opportunities to provide holistic and compassionate care to needy individuals. As spiritual leaders, we are often seen as trusted and respected figures within our communities, making us well-positioned to offer emotional support, spiritual guidance, and practical resources to struggling individuals. Ministry settings can also provide a sense of community, belonging, and connection to individuals who may feel isolated or marginalized in other spaces.

Another important strategy is to create a culture of empathy, compassion, and inclusivity within the ministry community. This involves fostering an environment where individuals feel accepted, supported, and valued for who they are, regardless of their background, beliefs, or struggles. Ministry leaders can promote open and honest communication, encourage vulnerability and authenticity, and provide opportunities for individuals to share their stories and experiences in a safe and non-judgmental space.

Furthermore, we can collaborate with mental health professionals, counselors, and community organizations to provide comprehensive support and resources to individuals in need. By building partnerships with external resources, ministry leaders can ensure that individuals receive the holistic care they need to address their trauma, mental health challenges, and emotional struggles. This may involve referring individuals to counseling services, support groups, crisis intervention programs, or other resources that can complement the spiritual and emotional support provided by the ministry.

Building partnerships with external community resources provides holistic care.

Creating safe and supportive environments for healing in ministry can have a profound impact on individuals' well-being, healing, and recovery. When individuals feel safe, supported, and empowered within the ministry setting, they are more likely to engage in their healing journey, seek help when needed, and experience positive outcomes in their mental health and spiritual growth. Safe and supportive environments can help individuals build resilience, develop coping skills, and foster a sense of hope and optimism for the future.

Research has shown that individuals who have access to safe and supportive environments are more likely to experience improvements in their mental health, spiritual well-being, and overall quality of life. They may report lower levels of anxiety, depression, and trauma symptoms and higher levels of satisfaction with their relationships, faith, and sense of purpose. Creating safe and supportive environments can also help reduce stigma, increase help-seeking behavior, and promote a sense of community among struggling individuals.

Chapter 10-Crisis Management

Whether it be natural disasters, personal tragedies, or societal upheavals, ministry leaders play a crucial role in offering spiritual, emotional, and practical assistance in times of crisis. However, the demands of crisis management can take a toll on our own well-being and mental health. Let's explore the importance of crisis management and self-care in ministry, the challenges and stressors faced by ministry leaders in times of crisis, strategies for effective crisis management and self-care, and the impact of self-care on ministry leaders' ability to navigate crises with resilience and compassion.

Importance of Self-Care in Crisis Management

Crisis management involves responding to unexpected events or situations that disrupt the normal functioning of individuals or communities. In times of crisis, ministry leaders are called upon to provide support, comfort, and guidance to those who are experiencing fear, grief, trauma, or loss. Effective crisis management involves assessing the needs of individuals and communities, offering practical assistance and resources, providing emotional support and counseling, and facilitating healing and recovery.

While taking care of others, the intensity of it all can cause us to lose sight of taking care of ourselves. Here is your reminder: Self-care is equally important in ministry, especially during times of crisis when the demands on ministry leaders can be overwhelming. Self-care involves taking intentional steps to prioritize one's own well-being, mental health, and resilience in order to effectively support others. By practicing self-care, ministry leaders can prevent burnout, compassion fatigue, and vicarious trauma, and maintain their capacity to provide compassionate and effective care to those in need.

Self-Care is equally important- especially during times of crisis.

Challenges and Stressors Faced by Ministry Leaders in Times of Crisis

Ministry leaders face a unique set of challenges and stressors when it comes to crisis management. In times of crisis, we may experience a heightened sense of responsibility, pressure, and emotional intensity as we navigate the needs of individuals and communities in distress. We may also face logistical challenges, resource constraints, and ethical dilemmas in providing support and assistance to those affected by the crisis.

Furthermore, we may experience personal stressors and triggers that can impact our ability to manage crises effectively. Witnessing the suffering and trauma of others, managing high levels of emotional intensity, and balancing the demands of ministry with personal commitments can take a toll on ministry leaders' mental health and well-being. Without proper self-care practices in place, we may drown while trying to rescue others.

Strategies for Effective Crisis Management and Self-Care

So, what self-care practices can we implement to avoid this? One key strategy is to establish clear protocols and procedures for crisis response within the ministry setting. This may involve creating a crisis response team, developing a communication plan, and identifying resources and support services for individuals in need.

Training and education are also important components of effective crisis management. Leaders can benefit from learning about trauma-informed care, crisis intervention techniques, and mental health first aid in order to better support individuals in crisis. By equipping ourselves with the necessary knowledge and skills, we can respond to crises with empathy, sensitivity, and effectiveness.

Ministry leaders can also benefit from incorporating self-care activities into our daily routines, such as mindfulness meditation, exercise, journaling, and seeking support from peers and mentors. Setting boundaries, practicing self-compassion, and seeking professional counseling or therapy when needed can also help us navigate the challenges of crisis management with grace and resilience.

Research has shown that leaders who engage in self-care practices report higher levels of job satisfaction, lower levels of burnout, and greater psychological well-being. By taking care of our own mental health and well-being, we are better equipped to support others in times of crisis and provide effective and compassionate care to those in need. Self-care not only benefits leaders personally but also enhances our ability to serve others with empathy, compassion, and resilience.

What Does the Bible Say About It?

Numerous Bible passages emphasize the importance of self-care and seeking solace in God during times of trouble. These teachings provide practical applications for implementing self-care strategies during times of high stress and crisis and emphasize the significance of faith and reliance on God in promoting overall well-being.

First, the Bible teaches that self-care is not a selfish act but rather a necessary component of fulfilling our responsibilities to ourselves and to others. 1 Corinthians 6:19-20 says, *"Do you not know that your bodies are temples of the Holy Spirit, who is in you, whom you have received from God? You are not your own; you were bought at a price. Therefore, honor God with your bodies."* This passage emphasizes the importance of taking care of our physical health as a way of honoring God and recognizing the divine significance of our bodies.

Moreover, in Matthew 11:28-30, Jesus says, *"Come to me, all you who are weary and burdened, and I will give you rest. Take my yoke upon you and learn from me, for I am gentle and humble in heart, and you will find rest for your souls. For my yoke is easy and my burden is light."* This highlights the invitation to seek refuge in God during times of distress and to find true rest in His presence.

In times of crisis, it can be easy to neglect self-care due to the overwhelming demands and pressures that we face. However, the Bible offers guidance on how to prioritize self-care even amidst chaos and uncertainty. Psalm 23:1-3 declares, *"The Lord is my shepherd, I lack nothing. He makes me lie down in green pastures, He leads me beside quiet waters, He refreshes my soul. He guides me along the right paths for his name's sake."* This passage illustrates the importance of finding moments of rest and rejuvenation in God's presence, even amid turmoil.

Ultimately, self-care from a biblical perspective is not just about tending to our physical and emotional needs but also about nurturing our spiritual connection with God. By anchoring ourselves in faith, prayer, and trust in God's providence, we can find strength, comfort, and hope during life's challenges. As we prioritize self-care and seek refuge in God's presence, we can navigate times of high stress and crisis with grace, resilience, and unwavering faith.

Supporting Others While Maintaining Personal Wellness

Supporting others is a noble and fulfilling endeavor deeply rooted in the teachings of the Bible. Throughout the Scriptures, there are numerous examples of individuals who offered their support, comfort, and encouragement to those in need. However, it is important to recognize the significance of maintaining personal well-being while extending support to others. Let's begin by exploring the biblical perspective on supporting others and self-care, examining the delicate balance between serving others and prioritizing one's own well-being.

Biblical Teachings on Supporting Others

One of the fundamental principles of Christianity is compassion for others. Galatians 6:2 says, *"Carry each other's burdens, and in this way, you will fulfill the law of Christ."* This passage emphasizes the importance of supporting and helping one another in times of need. Similarly, Proverbs 17:17 states, *"A friend loves at all times, and a brother is born for a time of adversity."* This verse underscores the value of being a faithful and supportive friend to others, especially during challenging circumstances.

Furthermore, 1 Thessalonians 5:11 says, *"Therefore encourage one another and build each other up, just as in fact you are doing."* This verse highlights the power of encouragement and uplifting one another through words and deeds. Supporting others is not only a commandment in the Bible but also a source of blessing and fulfillment for both the giver and the receiver.

Through love, compassion, self-care, and setting boundaries, we can fulfill our calling to support others in a way that honors God and promotes holistic well-being for ourselves.

Chapter 11-Ethical Considerations

Imagine this: You discover that a key member of your congregation—a trusted elder—is involved in unethical financial practices within the church. Confronting the issue risks fracturing the congregation and damaging your own reputation, yet remaining silent would compromise the integrity of the ministry and betray your ethical calling. This is the kind of ethical dilemma that can shake leaders to their core, forcing them to choose between protecting relationships and upholding the moral and spiritual values they vowed to defend. What do you do when doing the right thing could cost you everything? How do you manage the mental distress that it brings?

We are often faced with ethical dilemmas that can weigh heavily on our mental and emotional health. As we struggle with the complex intersection of faith, mental health, and ethics, we are charged with the responsibility of upholding the highest moral and ethical standards. The fact is that leaders who are emotionally and mentally healthy are more likely to make sound decisions.

Aligning Spiritual Guidance with Ethical Standards

Yes, we are entrusted with providing spiritual guidance while upholding ethical standards that respect the beliefs, values, and diversity of those we serve. This delicate balance requires sensitivity, discernment, and a commitment to integrity. Here are key aspects to consider when integrating spiritual guidance with ethical practices:

1. Respect for Individual Beliefs:
While we are often called to share our faith, it is essential to approach each individual with respect for their personal beliefs and values. In other words, we should avoid imposing our own spiritual convictions in a way that alienates or disrespects others. Instead, we must create an environment where people feel safe to explore and express their own faith journey, regardless of differences in doctrine or tradition.

2. Sensitivity to Diverse Perspectives:

In today's ministry settings, leaders encounter people from diverse cultural, religious, and philosophical backgrounds. An ethical approach requires sensitivity to these differences, recognizing that individuals' spiritual needs may be shaped by a variety of influences. We should strive to understand and honor these perspectives, offering support that affirms individuals' unique spiritual journeys rather than dismissing or undermining them.

3. Maintaining Boundaries:

Ethical ministry requires clear boundaries, particularly when offering spiritual counsel. We must ensure that our role as spiritual guides does not become coercive or manipulative. This includes being mindful of the power dynamics inherent in pastoral relationships and avoiding any actions or advice that might exploit or pressure individuals. For instance, a minister should not engage in personal or social relationships with individuals they are providing support to, as this can blur the lines of the therapeutic relationship and create conflicts of interest. Maintaining professional and personal boundaries safeguards both the leader and those seeking support.

4. Ethical Decision-Making:

We must ground our guidance in ethical decision-making processes that prioritize the well-being and autonomy of those we serve. This means helping individuals make choices that are in line with their own beliefs and values rather than dictating them. Leaders should offer spiritual insight while encouraging self-reflection and independent decision-making, ensuring that their advice empowers rather than controls.

5. Confidentiality and Trust:

Leaders are often privy to sensitive information shared in confidence. Upholding confidentiality is a foundational ethical responsibility, crucial for maintaining trust. We must guard personal information carefully, sharing only with consent or when it is ethically necessary to protect someone from harm.

> *Upholding confidentiality is a foundational ethical responsibility.*

Let's lean into this foundational element:

Confidentiality is a fundamental ethical principle in mental health promotion within ministry. Leaders must uphold the privacy and confidentiality of individuals seeking emotional and psychological support, ensuring that personal information is safeguarded. We should always operate within the bounds of professional discretion and seek appropriate consent before sharing personal details with other parties. Individuals seeking support from those in ministry must be able to trust that their personal information will be kept confidential. Breaching confidentiality can have serious consequences, eroding trust and potentially causing harm to those seeking support. For example, if a minister were to share confidential information about a parishioner's mental health struggles with others without their consent, it could lead to feelings of betrayal and could deter the individual from seeking further support.

Dual relationships, where the minister has multiple roles or relationships with the individual seeking support, can also present ethical challenges. While it is not always possible to avoid all dual relationships, we must be mindful of the potential for conflicts of interest and prioritize the well-being of the individual above all else. For example, if a minister is also the employer of an individual seeking support, they must take extra care to ensure that their dual roles do not influence the support they provide or compromise the individual's confidentiality.

Addressing Ethical Dilemmas. A Framework

Ethical dilemmas are unavoidable, but they are not unmanageable. Implementing ethical decision-making frameworks can help leaders navigate complex ethical dilemmas. These principles can guide your decision-making without depleting you in the process. For example, ethical principles such as autonomy, beneficence, non-maleficence, and justice can assist leaders in making sound decisions that prioritize their clients' well-being. Here's a brief description of each principle:

Ethical dilemmas are un-avoidable, but not un-manageable.

1. **Autonomy**: This principle emphasizes respecting individuals' right to make their own decisions, particularly regarding their spiritual and personal lives. Leaders should empower those they support to take ownership of their choices and respect their freedom to decide what aligns with their beliefs and values.

2. **Beneficence**: Beneficence calls for leaders to act in the best interest of those they serve, promoting well-being and doing good. Leaders should strive to provide support, guidance, and care that benefits

individuals, ensuring their spiritual, emotional, and physical welfare is considered.

3. **Non-Maleficence**: This principle focuses on avoiding harm. Leaders must ensure that their actions, guidance, or advice do not cause emotional, spiritual, or physical harm. Non-maleficence requires careful consideration to avoid unintentionally harming those seeking spiritual counsel.

4. **Justice**: Justice emphasizes fairness and equality, ensuring that all individuals receive equal treatment and opportunities for care, regardless of their background, beliefs, or status. Leaders must ensure that their support is unbiased and equitable, treating each person with respect and integrity.

By incorporating these principles into our decision-making process, we can ensure that our actions align with ethical standards and promote positive outcomes for those under our care.

Creating a Culture of Integrity

Finally, creating a culture of integrity is essential for effectively addressing ethical dilemmas. Leaders can foster an environment where ethical considerations are valued and prioritized by promoting open communication, transparency, and accountability. For example, leaders can establish regular training sessions on ethical guidelines, encourage team discussions on challenging ethical scenarios, and provide support for staff members facing ethical dilemmas.

Addressing ethical dilemmas is essential for promoting the well-being of members and upholding the values of faith-based organizations. By prioritizing ethical leadership, implementing decision-making frameworks, and cultivating a culture of integrity, leaders can navigate complex ethical situations with confidence and integrity. By emphasizing ethical principles and guidelines in our practice, we can enhance the quality of care provided to individuals seeking support in a religious context.

Chapter 12-Integration & Application of the Framework

As we conclude this journey into the mental health and well-being of leaders, it's important to outline a clear, practical framework that you can apply in your own leadership journey. This framework integrates the spiritual, emotional, and mental strategies discussed throughout the book, offering a holistic approach that supports leaders in maintaining balance and resilience. It is designed to be both a preventive and restorative guide, helping you thrive in your calling while caring for your mental well-being. Here is a summary of the key components of the framework:

1. Self-awareness and Emotional Intelligence. The first pillar of this framework is self-awareness. Leaders must consistently evaluate our emotional state and recognize our triggers. Emotional intelligence involves not only managing our own emotions but also understanding the emotions of those around us. By cultivating emotional intelligence and social awareness, leaders can create environments of trust, reduce conflict, and lead more effectively.

Practical Application:

- Engage in regular reflection practices, such as journaling or meditation.
- Seek feedback from trusted peers to understand how your leadership is affecting those around you.
- Practice mindfulness techniques to stay attuned to your emotions and responses during challenging situations.

2. Prioritize Self-Care. Self-care is essential to prevent burnout and maintain emotional stability. This means taking time for rest, engaging in activities that replenish your energy, and establishing routines that nurture both your body and mind. It's not just about physical health; it's about creating mental and spiritual space to recharge.

Practical Application:

- Create a balanced routine that includes exercise, sleep, and downtime for reflection and relaxation.

- Schedule a regular time for spiritual disciplines like prayer, worship, and study.
- Set aside "non-negotiable" personal time where you can step away from leadership responsibilities.

3. Build Resilience and Manage Stress. Resilience isn't about avoiding stress but learning to handle it in healthy ways. By developing coping mechanisms and building resilience, leaders can endure difficult seasons without becoming overwhelmed. This involves not only managing day-to-day stress but also preparing for crises with a clear, resilient mindset.

Practical Application:
- Develop a stress-management plan that includes coping strategies such as deep breathing, exercise, and taking breaks when overwhelmed.
- Practice gratitude and positive thinking to shift your mindset in moments of stress.
- Regularly debrief with a trusted mentor or counselor to release accumulated stress.

4. Create a Supportive Community. One of the most important aspects of this framework is the creation of a trusted community where you can be vulnerable. Whether it's a small group of peers, a mentor, or a counselor, you need spaces where you can safely express your struggles and be poured into without judgment.

Practical Application:

- Actively seek out and engage with a support network that allows for vulnerability and openness.
- Participate in peer groups where leaders can share experiences, learn from each other, and offer mutual support.
- Pursue mentoring relationships where someone pours into you and guides your personal and professional growth.

5. Address Stigma and Seek Help When Needed. Leaders often hesitate to seek help due to the stigma around mental health. However, recognizing when you need assistance is a mark of strength, not weakness. This framework encourages leaders to break the silence and seek professional support when needed, ensuring that we can continue leading from a place of health and wholeness.

Practical Application:

- Normalize the conversation around mental health within your leadership circles.
- Seek therapy or counseling as a preventive measure, not just when in crisis.

- Encourage a culture within your organization that supports mental health, making it easier for others to seek help too.

6. Set Boundaries and Foster Health Relationships. Boundaries are crucial to leading effectively and sustaining well-being. Leaders must learn to say "no" to certain demands to protect our time and emotional health. At the same time, cultivating healthy relationships is key to maintaining emotional balance and avoiding isolation.

Practical Application:
- Set clear boundaries in your schedule to protect your personal time and mental space.
- Foster transparent, healthy communication in both your personal and professional relationships.
- Regularly assess your relationships to ensure they are mutually supportive and not draining.

7. Integrate Spiritual and Mental Well-Being. Lastly, spiritual well-being is deeply intertwined with mental health. Leaders who nurture their spiritual lives find greater clarity and peace, which can enhance their mental and emotional resilience. This framework encourages us to **maintain strong spiritual practices** to sustain our mental health.

Practical Application:

- Maintain a consistent practice of prayer, reflection, and spiritual study.
- Participate in corporate worship and spiritual retreats to deepen your connection with God.
- Reflect on scripture and theological insights as sources of guidance during difficult times.

This framework isn't just a guide—it's a lifeline. The pressures of leadership can pull you in every direction, but following this blueprint will save your sanity. It gives you clarity when everything feels chaotic, equips you with practical tools to manage stress, and provides the spiritual grounding you need to stand firm. Don't wait until you're on the verge of burnout or overwhelmed by the weight of your calling. Use this framework now—it will protect your mind, restore your strength, and help you lead with greater purpose, focus, and resilience. Your well-being is worth it!

This framework isn't just a guide...
It's a LIFELINE!

Conclusion

A Sustainable Approach to Leadership

Let's face it—the weight of leadership can be heavy! So many lives are at stake, including our own. Many start out strong but become crushed by the weight of the mantle. It doesn't mean they weren't called. It doesn't mean they were weak. It just means the weight is heavy, and without the proper support, it is impossible to sustain.

By following this framework, you can establish a sustainable approach to your mental and emotional well-being. Leadership is a journey that requires both strength and vulnerability. By prioritizing self-care, building support systems, and seeking help when needed, you can continue to fulfill your divine calling without sacrificing your health. Remember, you are not meant to walk this path alone. Embrace the framework and lead from a place of wholeness.

About the Author

Dwayne is married to Esther Marcellus-Perry. He is a dedicated servant of Christ and passionate about empowering individuals to reach their full potential. With a heart rooted in love and a deep desire to see others thrive, he serves others out of an apostolic anointing. Driven by a genuine love for people, Dwayne seeks to uplift and inspire through coaching, mentoring, writings, teachings, and ministry.

Dwayne is a remarkable individual who has attained his Doctorate in Education and Ministry. His life's journey has been marked by excellence, service, education, and a deep commitment to empowering others. With a career spanning 13 years as a professional basketball player, Dwayne's passion for sports and his unwavering dedication to his craft have shaped him into the person he is today. Beyond his achievements on the court, Dwayne's true calling lies in his ability to serve others out of an apostolic anointing. Recognized as an anointed teacher, he possesses a unique gift for imparting wisdom and inspiring transformation in the lives of those he encounters. Through his teachings, Dwayne has touched countless hearts, helping individuals unlock their full potential and discover their purpose. As a coach, mentor, and developer of people, he has made it his mission to guide others on their journey toward personal and professional growth.

His commitment to nurturing talent and fostering a spirit of excellence has earned him the respect and admiration of those he has had the privilege to work with. Dwayne's ability to see the potential in others and empower them to reach new heights is a testament to his servant-hearted nature.

In addition to his athletic and teaching prowess, Dwayne is a sought-after speaker and motivator. His captivating presence and ability to connect with diverse audiences make him a powerful force for change. Through his engaging talks, he challenges individuals to overcome obstacles, embrace their unique gifts, and live a life of purpose and significance. His life experiences, both on and off the court, have shaped his character and fueled his passion for making a positive impact. His unwavering commitment to serving others, combined with his natural leadership abilities, have positioned him as a catalyst for transformation in the lives of many.

As you embark on this journey through the pages of this book, allow Dwayne's wisdom, insights, and experiences to inspire and empower you. His unique blend of athletic prowess, spiritual anointing, and dedication to developing people will undoubtedly leave a lasting impact on your life. Prepare to be challenged, motivated, and equipped as you delve into the transformative teachings of Dr. Dwayne C. Perry, a former professional basketball player, an anointed teacher, a coach, mentor, and a developer of people.

Notes

1. BBC News. "Sandeep Rehal's Story." BBC News, 14 Jan. 2019, www.bbc.com/news/uk-england-46864749.

2. The Guardian. "Jacinda Ardern's Resignation." The Guardian, 19 Jan. 2023, www.theguardian.com/world/2023/jan/19/jacinda-ardern-resigns-new-zealand-prime-minister.

3. The Washington Post. "Pastor Andrew Stoecklein's Death." The Washington Post, 28 Aug. 2018, www.washingtonpost.com/news/acts-of-faith/wp/2018/08/28/megachurch-pastor-took-his-own-life-after-battle-with-mental-illness-leaving-his-congregation-stunned/.

4. CNN. "Pastor Jarrid Wilson's Advocacy and Tragic Death." CNN, 10 Sept. 2019, www.cnn.com/2019/09/10/us/pastor-jarrid-wilson-suicide/index.html.

5. Cloud, Henry. *Boundaries: When to Say Yes, How to Say No to Take Control of Your Life*. Grand Rapids: Zondervan, 1992